Who Gives a Fuck!

A GRATITUDE JOURNAL
FOR BAD ASS WOMEN

Goldstar Journals

This fucking journal belongs to:

IF THAT ISN'T YOU STAY THE FUCK OUT!

Welcome to
the shit show!

ONE GOOD
FUCKING THING
THAT HAPPENED
TODAY IS ....

DATE: _____

I AM SO
FUCKING
GRATEFUL FOR

_____
_____
_____
_____

SHIT I HAVE
TO DO TODAY

- [ ] _____
- [ ] _____
- [ ] _____
- [ ] _____
- [ ] _____
- [ ] _____

ANOTHER KICK ASS DAY!

I'M SO GLAD I DIDN'T FUCKING DO THIS TODAY .....

DICKHEAD OF THE DAY

_____
_____
_____
_____

HOW MANY PEOPLE PISSED ME OFF TODAY?

(CIRCLE A CUPCAKE FOR EACH PERSON)

♥ NOTES & SHIT

_____
_____
_____
_____
_____
_____
_____
_____
_____
_____
_____
_____

I'M SO FUCKING PROUD OF MYSELF FOR THIS.....

IF TODAY SUCKED...LET THAT SHIT GO!

ONE GOOD
FUCKING THING
THAT HAPPENED
TODAY IS ....

DATE: _____

I AM SO
FUCKING
GRATEFUL FOR

SHIT I HAVE
TO DO TODAY

- [ ]
- [ ]
- [ ]
- [ ]
- [ ]
- [ ]

ANOTHER KICK ASS DAY!

I'M SO GLAD I DIDN'T FUCKING DO THIS TODAY .....

BITCH OF THE DAY

_____

_____

_____

_____

HOW MANY PEOPLE PISSED ME OFF TODAY?

(CIRCLE A CUPCAKE FOR EACH PERSON)

♥ NOTES & SHIT

_____
_____
_____
_____
_____
_____
_____
_____
_____
_____
_____

I'M SO FUCKING PROUD OF MYSELF FOR THIS.....

DON'T WORRY. BE FUCKING HAPPY AND SHIT!

ONE GOOD
FUCKING THING
THAT HAPPENED
TODAY IS ....

DATE: _____

I AM SO
FUCKING
GRATEFUL FOR

SHIT I HAVE
TO DO TODAY

- [ ]
- [ ]
- [ ]
- [ ]
- [ ]
- [ ]

ANOTHER KICK ASS DAY!

I'M SO GLAD I DIDN'T FUCKING DO THIS TODAY .....

ASSHOLE OF THE DAY

HOW MANY PEOPLE PISSED ME OFF TODAY?

(CIRCLE A CUPCAKE FOR EACH PERSON)

_____
_____
_____
_____

♥ NOTES & SHIT

_____
_____
_____
_____
_____
_____
_____
_____
_____
_____
_____

I'M SO FUCKING PROUD OF MYSELF FOR THIS.....

GET OUT THERE TOMORROW AND MAKE LIFE YOUR BITCH!

ONE GOOD
FUCKING THING
THAT HAPPENED
TODAY IS ....

DATE: _____

I AM SO
FUCKING
GRATEFUL FOR

_____

_____

_____

_____

_____

SHIT I HAVE
TO DO TODAY

- [ ] _____
- [ ] _____
- [ ] _____
- [ ] _____
- [ ] _____
- [ ] _____

ANOTHER KICK ASS DAY!

I'M SO GLAD I DIDN'T FUCKING DO THIS TODAY .....

JERK OF THE DAY

HOW MANY PEOPLE PISSED ME OFF TODAY?
(CIRCLE A CUPCAKE FOR EACH PERSON)

♥ NOTES & SHIT

I'M SO FUCKING PROUD OF MYSELF FOR THIS.....

YOU'RE AMAZING. KEEP THAT SHIT UP!

ONE GOOD FUCKING THING THAT HAPPENED TODAY IS ......

DATE: _____

I AM SO FUCKING GRATEFUL FOR

_____
_____
_____
_____
_____

SHIT I HAVE TO DO TODAY

- [ ] _____
- [ ] _____
- [ ] _____
- [ ] _____
- [ ] _____
- [ ] _____

ANOTHER KICK ASS DAY!

I'M SO GLAD I DIDN'T FUCKING DO THIS TODAY .....

JACKASS OF THE DAY

_____
_____
_____
_____

HOW MANY PEOPLE PISSED ME OFF TODAY?

(CIRCLE A CUPCAKE FOR EACH PERSON)

 # NOTES & SHIT

_____
_____
_____
_____
_____
_____
_____
_____
_____
_____

FUCK THIS SHIT SHOW!

I'M SO FUCKING PROUD OF MYSELF FOR THIS.....

ONE GOOD FUCKING THING THAT HAPPENED TODAY IS ....

DATE: _____

I AM SO FUCKING GRATEFUL FOR

_____
_____
_____
_____

SHIT I HAVE TO DO TODAY

- [ ] _____
- [ ] _____
- [ ] _____
- [ ] _____
- [ ] _____
- [ ] _____

ANOTHER KICK ASS DAY!

I'M SO GLAD I DIDN'T FUCKING DO THIS TODAY .....

DICKHEAD OF THE DAY

_____
_____
_____
_____

HOW MANY PEOPLE PISSED ME OFF TODAY?

(CIRCLE A CUPCAKE FOR EACH PERSON)

♥ NOTES & SHIT

_____
_____
_____
_____
_____
_____
_____
_____
_____
_____

I'M SO FUCKING PROUD OF MYSELF FOR THIS.....

IF TODAY SUCKED...LET THAT SHIT GO!

ONE GOOD FUCKING THING THAT HAPPENED TODAY IS ....

DATE: _____

I AM SO FUCKING GRATEFUL FOR

_____
_____
_____
_____
_____

SHIT I HAVE TO DO TODAY

- [ ] _____
- [ ] _____
- [ ] _____
- [ ] _____
- [ ] _____
- [ ] _____

ANOTHER KICK ASS DAY!

I'M SO GLAD I DIDN'T FUCKING DO THIS TODAY .....

BITCH OF THE DAY

HOW MANY PEOPLE PISSED ME OFF TODAY?

(CIRCLE A CUPCAKE FOR EACH PERSON)

♥ *NOTES & SHIT*

I'M SO FUCKING PROUD OF MYSELF FOR THIS.....

DON'T WORRY. BE FUCKING HAPPY AND SHIT!

ONE GOOD
FUCKING THING
THAT HAPPENED
TODAY IS ....

DATE: _____

I AM SO
FUCKING
GRATEFUL FOR

_____

_____

_____

_____

_____

SHIT I HAVE
TO DO TODAY

- [ ] _____
- [ ] _____
- [ ] _____
- [ ] _____
- [ ] _____
- [ ] _____

ANOTHER KICK ASS DAY!

I'M SO GLAD I DIDN'T FUCKING DO THIS TODAY .....

ASSHOLE OF THE DAY

_____
_____
_____
_____

HOW MANY PEOPLE PISSED ME OFF TODAY?

(CIRCLE A CUPCAKE FOR EACH PERSON)

 # NOTES & SHIT

_____
_____
_____
_____
_____
_____
_____
_____
_____
_____
_____

I'M SO FUCKING PROUD OF MYSELF FOR THIS.....

GET OUT THERE TOMORROW AND MAKE LIFE YOUR BITCH!

ONE GOOD
FUCKING THING
THAT HAPPENED
TODAY IS ....

DATE: _____

I AM SO FUCKING GRATEFUL FOR

_____

_____

_____

_____

_____

SHIT I HAVE TO DO TODAY

- [ ] _____
- [ ] _____
- [ ] _____
- [ ] _____
- [ ] _____
- [ ] _____

ANOTHER KICK ASS DAY!

I'M SO GLAD I DIDN'T FUCKING DO THIS TODAY .....

JERK OF THE DAY

HOW MANY PEOPLE PISSED ME OFF TODAY?

(CIRCLE A CUPCAKE FOR EACH PERSON)

 ## NOTES & SHIT

I'M SO FUCKING PROUD OF MYSELF FOR THIS.....

YOU'RE AMAZING. KEEP THAT SHIT UP!

ONE GOOD FUCKING THING THAT HAPPENED TODAY IS ....

DATE: _____

I AM SO FUCKING GRATEFUL FOR

_____
_____
_____
_____
_____

SHIT I HAVE TO DO TODAY

☐ _____
☐ _____
☐ _____
☐ _____
☐ _____
☐ _____

ANOTHER KICK ASS DAY!

I'M SO GLAD I DIDN'T FUCKING DO THIS TODAY .....

JACKASS OF THE DAY

_____
_____
_____
_____
_____

HOW MANY PEOPLE PISSED ME OFF TODAY?

(CIRCLE A CUPCAKE FOR EACH PERSON)

♥ *NOTES & SHIT*

_____
_____
_____
_____
_____
_____
_____
_____
_____
_____

FUCK THIS SHIT SHOW!

I'M SO FUCKING PROUD OF MYSELF FOR THIS.....

DATE: _ _ _ _ _ _ _ _ _ _ _ _ _

I AM SO FUCKING GRATEFUL FOR

_____

_____

_____

_____

SHIT I HAVE TO DO TODAY

- [ ] _____
- [ ] _____
- [ ] _____
- [ ] _____
- [ ] _____
- [ ] _____

ANOTHER KICK ASS DAY!

I'M SO GLAD I DIDN'T FUCKING DO THIS TODAY .....

BITCH OF THE DAY

HOW MANY PEOPLE PISSED ME OFF TODAY?

(CIRCLE A CUPCAKE FOR EACH PERSON)

♥ NOTES & SHIT

I'M SO FUCKING PROUD OF MYSELF FOR THIS.....

DON'T WORRY. BE FUCKING HAPPY AND SHIT!

ONE GOOD FUCKING THING THAT HAPPENED TODAY IS ....

DATE: _____

I AM SO FUCKING GRATEFUL FOR

_____
_____
_____
_____
_____

SHIT I HAVE TO DO TODAY

- [ ] _____
- [ ] _____
- [ ] _____
- [ ] _____
- [ ] _____
- [ ] _____

ANOTHER KICK ASS DAY!

I'M SO GLAD I DIDN'T FUCKING DO THIS TODAY .....

DICKHEAD OF THE DAY

HOW MANY PEOPLE PISSED ME OFF TODAY?

(CIRCLE A CUPCAKE FOR EACH PERSON)

 NOTES & SHIT

I'M SO FUCKING PROUD OF MYSELF FOR THIS.....

IF TODAY SUCKED...LET THAT SHIT GO!

ONE GOOD
FUCKING THING
THAT HAPPENED
TODAY IS ....

DATE: _ _ _ _ _ _ _ _ _ _ _ _ _ _

I AM SO
FUCKING
GRATEFUL FOR

_____

_____

_____

_____

_____

SHIT I HAVE
TO DO TODAY

- [ ] _____
- [ ] _____
- [ ] _____
- [ ] _____
- [ ] _____
- [ ] _____

ANOTHER KICK ASS DAY!

I'M SO GLAD I DIDN'T FUCKING DO THIS TODAY .....

BITCH OF THE DAY

HOW MANY PEOPLE PISSED ME OFF TODAY?

(CIRCLE A CUPCAKE FOR EACH PERSON)

♥ NOTES & SHIT

I'M SO FUCKING PROUD OF MYSELF FOR THIS.....

DON'T WORRY. BE FUCKING HAPPY AND SHIT!

DATE: _____

I AM SO FUCKING GRATEFUL FOR

_____

_____

_____

_____

_____

SHIT I HAVE TO DO TODAY

- [ ] _____
- [ ] _____
- [ ] _____
- [ ] _____
- [ ] _____
- [ ] _____

ANOTHER KICK ASS DAY!

I'M SO GLAD I DIDN'T FUCKING DO THIS TODAY .....

ASSHOLE OF THE DAY

_____
_____
_____
_____

HOW MANY PEOPLE PISSED ME OFF TODAY?

(CIRCLE A CUPCAKE FOR EACH PERSON)

♥ NOTES & SHIT

_____
_____
_____
_____
_____
_____
_____
_____
_____
_____
_____

I'M SO FUCKING PROUD OF MYSELF FOR THIS.....

GET OUT THERE TOMORROW AND MAKE LIFE YOUR BITCH!

DATE: _____

I AM SO FUCKING GRATEFUL FOR

_____

_____

_____

_____

_____

SHIT I HAVE TO DO TODAY

- [ ] _____
- [ ] _____
- [ ] _____
- [ ] _____
- [ ] _____
- [ ] _____

ANOTHER KICK ASS DAY!

I'M SO GLAD I DIDN'T FUCKING DO THIS TODAY .....

JERK OF THE DAY

_____
_____
_____
_____

HOW MANY PEOPLE PISSED ME OFF TODAY?

(CIRCLE A CUPCAKE FOR EACH PERSON)

♥ **NOTES & SHIT**

_____
_____
_____
_____
_____
_____
_____
_____
_____
_____
_____
_____

I'M SO FUCKING PROUD OF MYSELF FOR THIS.....

YOU'RE AMAZING. KEEP THAT SHIT UP!

ONE GOOD FUCKING THING THAT HAPPENED TODAY IS ....

DATE: _____

I AM SO FUCKING GRATEFUL FOR

_____
_____
_____
_____

SHIT I HAVE TO DO TODAY

☐ _____
☐ _____
☐ _____
☐ _____
☐ _____
☐ _____

ANOTHER KICK ASS DAY!

I'M SO GLAD I DIDN'T FUCKING DO THIS TODAY .....

JACKASS OF THE DAY

_____
_____
_____
_____

HOW MANY PEOPLE PISSED ME OFF TODAY?

(CIRCLE A CUPCAKE FOR EACH PERSON)

♥ **NOTES & SHIT**

_____
_____
_____
_____
_____
_____
_____
_____
_____
_____
_____

FUCK THIS SHIT SHOW!

I'M SO FUCKING PROUD OF MYSELF FOR THIS.....

ONE GOOD
FUCKING THING
THAT HAPPENED
TODAY IS ....

DATE: _____

I AM SO
FUCKING
GRATEFUL FOR

_____
_____
_____
_____

SHIT I HAVE
TO DO TODAY

- [ ] _____
- [ ] _____
- [ ] _____
- [ ] _____
- [ ] _____
- [ ] _____

ANOTHER KICK ASS DAY!

I'M SO GLAD I DIDN'T FUCKING DO THIS TODAY .....

ASSHOLE OF THE DAY

HOW MANY PEOPLE PISSED ME OFF TODAY?

(CIRCLE A CUPCAKE FOR EACH PERSON)

 NOTES & SHIT

I'M SO FUCKING PROUD OF MYSELF FOR THIS.....

GET OUT THERE TOMORROW AND MAKE LIFE YOUR BITCH!

ONE GOOD
FUCKING THING
THAT HAPPENED
TODAY IS ....

DATE: _____

I AM SO
FUCKING
GRATEFUL FOR

_____
_____
_____
_____
_____

SHIT I HAVE
TO DO TODAY

☐ _____
☐ _____
☐ _____
☐ _____
☐ _____
☐ _____

ANOTHER KICK ASS DAY!

I'M SO GLAD I DIDN'T FUCKING DO THIS TODAY .....

DICKHEAD OF THE DAY

HOW MANY PEOPLE PISSED ME OFF TODAY?

(CIRCLE A CUPCAKE FOR EACH PERSON)

 # NOTES & SHIT

I'M SO FUCKING PROUD OF MYSELF FOR THIS.....

IF TODAY SUCKED...LET THAT SHIT GO!

ONE GOOD
FUCKING THING
THAT HAPPENED
TODAY IS ....

DATE: _____

I AM SO FUCKING GRATEFUL FOR

_____
_____
_____
_____
_____

SHIT I HAVE TO DO TODAY

- [ ] _____
- [ ] _____
- [ ] _____
- [ ] _____
- [ ] _____
- [ ] _____

ANOTHER KICK ASS DAY!

I'M SO GLAD I DIDN'T FUCKING DO THIS TODAY .....

BITCH OF THE DAY

HOW MANY PEOPLE PISSED ME OFF TODAY?

(CIRCLE A CUPCAKE FOR EACH PERSON)

 # NOTES & SHIT

I'M SO FUCKING PROUD OF MYSELF FOR THIS.....

DON'T WORRY. BE FUCKING HAPPY AND SHIT!

ONE GOOD FUCKING THING THAT HAPPENED TODAY IS ....

DATE: _____

I AM SO FUCKING GRATEFUL FOR

_____

_____

_____

_____

SHIT I HAVE TO DO TODAY

- [ ] _____
- [ ] _____
- [ ] _____
- [ ] _____
- [ ] _____
- [ ] _____

ANOTHER KICK ASS DAY!

I'M SO GLAD I DIDN'T FUCKING DO THIS TODAY .....

ASSHOLE OF THE DAY

HOW MANY PEOPLE PISSED ME OFF TODAY?

(CIRCLE A CUPCAKE FOR EACH PERSON)

 NOTES & SHIT

I'M SO FUCKING PROUD OF MYSELF FOR THIS.....

GET OUT THERE TOMORROW AND MAKE LIFE YOUR BITCH!

DATE: _____

I AM SO FUCKING GRATEFUL FOR

_____
_____
_____
_____
_____

SHIT I HAVE TO DO TODAY

☐ _____
☐ _____
☐ _____
☐ _____
☐ _____
☐ _____

ANOTHER KICK ASS DAY!

I'M SO GLAD I DIDN'T FUCKING DO THIS TODAY.....

JERK OF THE DAY

HOW MANY PEOPLE PISSED ME OFF TODAY?

(CIRCLE A CUPCAKE FOR EACH PERSON)

 ## NOTES & SHIT

I'M SO FUCKING PROUD OF MYSELF FOR THIS.....

YOU'RE AMAZING. KEEP THAT SHIT UP!

ONE GOOD FUCKING THING THAT HAPPENED TODAY IS ....

DATE: _____

I AM SO FUCKING GRATEFUL FOR

_____

_____

_____

_____

_____

SHIT I HAVE TO DO TODAY

- [ ] _____
- [ ] _____
- [ ] _____
- [ ] _____
- [ ] _____
- [ ] _____

ANOTHER KICK ASS DAY!

I'M SO GLAD I DIDN'T FUCKING DO THIS TODAY .....

JACKASS OF THE DAY

HOW MANY PEOPLE PISSED ME OFF TODAY?

(CIRCLE A CUPCAKE FOR EACH PERSON)

_____
_____
_____
_____

♥ NOTES & SHIT

_____
_____
_____
_____
_____
_____
_____
_____
_____
_____
_____

I'M SO FUCKING PROUD OF MYSELF FOR THIS.....

FUCK THIS SHIT SHOW!

ONE GOOD
FUCKING THING
THAT HAPPENED
TODAY IS ....

DATE: _____

I AM SO FUCKING GRATEFUL FOR

_____
_____
_____
_____

SHIT I HAVE TO DO TODAY

- [ ] _____
- [ ] _____
- [ ] _____
- [ ] _____
- [ ] _____
- [ ] _____

ANOTHER KICK ASS DAY!

I'M SO GLAD I DIDN'T FUCKING DO THIS TODAY .....

ASSHOLE OF THE DAY

HOW MANY PEOPLE PISSED ME OFF TODAY?

(CIRCLE A CUPCAKE FOR EACH PERSON)

♥ NOTES & SHIT

I'M SO FUCKING PROUD OF MYSELF FOR THIS.....

GET OUT THERE TOMORROW AND MAKE LIFE YOUR BITCH!

ONE GOOD FUCKING THING THAT HAPPENED TODAY IS ....

DATE: _____

I AM SO FUCKING GRATEFUL FOR

_____
_____
_____
_____
_____

SHIT I HAVE TO DO TODAY

- [ ] _____
- [ ] _____
- [ ] _____
- [ ] _____
- [ ] _____
- [ ] _____

ANOTHER KICK ASS DAY!

I'M SO GLAD I DIDN'T FUCKING DO THIS TODAY .....

DICKHEAD OF THE DAY

HOW MANY PEOPLE PISSED ME OFF TODAY?

(CIRCLE A CUPCAKE FOR EACH PERSON)

 NOTES & SHIT

I'M SO FUCKING PROUD OF MYSELF FOR THIS.....

IF TODAY SUCKED...LET THAT SHIT GO!

ONE GOOD FUCKING THING THAT HAPPENED TODAY IS ....

DATE: _____

I AM SO FUCKING GRATEFUL FOR

SHIT I HAVE TO DO TODAY

- [ ]
- [ ]
- [ ]
- [ ]
- [ ]
- [ ]

ANOTHER KICK ASS DAY!

I'M SO GLAD I DIDN'T FUCKING DO THIS TODAY .....

BITCH OF THE DAY

HOW MANY PEOPLE PISSED ME OFF TODAY?

(CIRCLE A CUPCAKE FOR EACH PERSON)

 NOTES & SHIT

I'M SO FUCKING PROUD OF MYSELF FOR THIS.....

DON'T WORRY. BE FUCKING HAPPY AND SHIT!

ONE GOOD FUCKING THING THAT HAPPENED TODAY IS ....

DATE: _____

I AM SO FUCKING GRATEFUL FOR

_____
_____
_____
_____
_____

SHIT I HAVE TO DO TODAY

- [ ] _____
- [ ] _____
- [ ] _____
- [ ] _____
- [ ] _____
- [ ] _____

ANOTHER KICK ASS DAY!

I'M SO GLAD I DIDN'T FUCKING DO THIS TODAY .....

ASSHOLE OF THE DAY

HOW MANY PEOPLE PISSED ME OFF TODAY?

(CIRCLE A CUPCAKE FOR EACH PERSON)

♥ NOTES & SHIT

I'M SO FUCKING PROUD OF MYSELF FOR THIS.....

GET OUT THERE TOMORROW AND MAKE LIFE YOUR BITCH!

ONE GOOD
FUCKING THING
THAT HAPPENED
TODAY IS ....

DATE: _____

I AM SO FUCKING GRATEFUL FOR

SHIT I HAVE TO DO TODAY

ANOTHER KICK ASS DAY!

I'M SO GLAD I DIDN'T FUCKING DO THIS TODAY.....

JERK OF THE DAY

_____
_____
_____
_____

HOW MANY PEOPLE PISSED ME OFF TODAY?

(CIRCLE A CUPCAKE FOR EACH PERSON)

♥ NOTES & SHIT

_____
_____
_____
_____
_____
_____
_____
_____
_____
_____

I'M SO FUCKING PROUD OF MYSELF FOR THIS.....

YOU'RE AMAZING. KEEP THAT SHIT UP!

ONE GOOD
FUCKING THING
THAT HAPPENED
TODAY IS ....

DATE: _____

I AM SO FUCKING GRATEFUL FOR

_____

_____

_____

_____

SHIT I HAVE TO DO TODAY

- [ ] _____
- [ ] _____
- [ ] _____
- [ ] _____
- [ ] _____
- [ ] _____

ANOTHER KICK ASS DAY!

I'M SO GLAD I DIDN'T FUCKING DO THIS TODAY .....

JACKASS OF THE DAY

HOW MANY PEOPLE PISSED ME OFF TODAY?

(CIRCLE A CUPCAKE FOR EACH PERSON)

NOTES & SHIT

I'M SO FUCKING PROUD OF MYSELF FOR THIS.....

FUCK THIS SHIT SHOW!

ONE GOOD
FUCKING THING
THAT HAPPENED
TODAY IS ....

DATE: _____

I AM SO FUCKING GRATEFUL FOR

SHIT I HAVE TO DO TODAY

- [ ]
- [ ]
- [ ]
- [ ]
- [ ]
- [ ]

ANOTHER KICK ASS DAY!

I'M SO GLAD I DIDN'T FUCKING DO THIS TODAY .....

BITCH OF THE DAY

_____
_____
_____
_____

HOW MANY PEOPLE PISSED ME OFF TODAY?

(CIRCLE A CUPCAKE FOR EACH PERSON)

♥ NOTES & SHIT

_____
_____
_____
_____
_____
_____
_____
_____
_____
_____

I'M SO FUCKING PROUD OF MYSELF FOR THIS.....

DON'T WORRY. BE FUCKING HAPPY AND SHIT!

ONE GOOD
FUCKING THING
THAT HAPPENED
TODAY IS ....

DATE: _____

I AM SO FUCKING GRATEFUL FOR

_____

_____

_____

_____

SHIT I HAVE TO DO TODAY

- [ ] _____
- [ ] _____
- [ ] _____
- [ ] _____
- [ ] _____
- [ ] _____

ANOTHER KICK ASS DAY!

I'M SO GLAD I DIDN'T FUCKING DO THIS TODAY .....

DICKHEAD OF THE DAY

_____
_____
_____
_____

HOW MANY PEOPLE PISSED ME OFF TODAY?

(CIRCLE A CUPCAKE FOR EACH PERSON)

♥ NOTES & SHIT

_____
_____
_____
_____
_____
_____
_____
_____
_____
_____
_____

I'M SO FUCKING PROUD OF MYSELF FOR THIS.....

IF TODAY SUCKED...LET THAT SHIT GO!

ONE GOOD
FUCKING THING
THAT HAPPENED
TODAY IS ....

DATE: _____

I AM SO FUCKING GRATEFUL FOR

_____
_____
_____
_____

SHIT I HAVE TO DO TODAY

☐ _____
☐ _____
☐ _____
☐ _____
☐ _____
☐ _____

ANOTHER KICK ASS DAY!

I'M SO GLAD I DIDN'T FUCKING DO THIS TODAY .....

BITCH OF THE DAY

HOW MANY PEOPLE PISSED ME OFF TODAY?

(CIRCLE A CUPCAKE FOR EACH PERSON)

 # NOTES & SHIT

I'M SO FUCKING PROUD OF MYSELF FOR THIS.....

DON'T WORRY. BE FUCKING HAPPY AND SHIT!

DATE: _____

I AM SO FUCKING GRATEFUL FOR

_____

_____

_____

_____

SHIT I HAVE TO DO TODAY

☐ _____

☐ _____

☐ _____

☐ _____

☐ _____

☐ _____

ANOTHER KICK ASS DAY!

I'M SO GLAD I DIDN'T FUCKING DO THIS TODAY .....

ASSHOLE OF THE DAY

HOW MANY PEOPLE PISSED ME OFF TODAY?

(CIRCLE A CUPCAKE FOR EACH PERSON)

 NOTES & SHIT

I'M SO FUCKING PROUD OF MYSELF FOR THIS.....

GET OUT THERE TOMORROW AND MAKE LIFE YOUR BITCH!

ONE GOOD
FUCKING THING
THAT HAPPENED
TODAY IS ....

DATE: _ _ _ _ _ _ _ _ _ _ _

I AM SO
FUCKING
GRATEFUL FOR

_____
_____
_____
_____
_____

SHIT I HAVE
TO DO TODAY

- [ ] _____
- [ ] _____
- [ ] _____
- [ ] _____
- [ ] _____
- [ ] _____

ANOTHER KICK ASS DAY!

I'M SO GLAD I DIDN'T FUCKING DO THIS TODAY .....

JERK OF THE DAY

HOW MANY PEOPLE PISSED ME OFF TODAY?

(CIRCLE A CUPCAKE FOR EACH PERSON)

_____
_____
_____
_____

♥ NOTES & SHIT

_____
_____
_____
_____
_____
_____
_____
_____
_____
_____
_____

I'M SO FUCKING PROUD OF MYSELF FOR THIS.....

YOU'RE AMAZING. KEEP THAT SHIT UP!

DATE: _____

I AM SO FUCKING GRATEFUL FOR

_____
_____
_____
_____

SHIT I HAVE TO DO TODAY

- [ ] _____
- [ ] _____
- [ ] _____
- [ ] _____
- [ ] _____
- [ ] _____

ANOTHER KICK ASS DAY!

I'M SO GLAD I DIDN'T FUCKING DO THIS TODAY .....

JACKASS OF THE DAY

HOW MANY PEOPLE PISSED ME OFF TODAY?

(CIRCLE A CUPCAKE FOR EACH PERSON)

 # NOTES & SHIT

I'M SO FUCKING PROUD OF MYSELF FOR THIS.....

FUCK THIS SHIT SHOW!

DATE: _____

I AM SO
FUCKING
GRATEFUL FOR

SHIT I HAVE
TO DO TODAY

ANOTHER KICK ASS DAY!

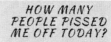

I'M SO GLAD I DIDN'T FUCKING DO THIS TODAY .....

JERK OF THE DAY

_____
_____
_____
_____
_____

HOW MANY PEOPLE PISSED ME OFF TODAY?

(CIRCLE A CUPCAKE FOR EACH PERSON)

 # NOTES & SHIT

_____
_____
_____
_____
_____
_____
_____
_____
_____
_____

I'M SO FUCKING PROUD OF MYSELF FOR THIS.....

YOU'RE AMAZING. KEEP THAT SHIT UP!

DATE: _____

I AM SO FUCKING GRATEFUL FOR

_____

_____

_____

_____

SHIT I HAVE TO DO TODAY

- [ ] _____
- [ ] _____
- [ ] _____
- [ ] _____
- [ ] _____
- [ ] _____

ANOTHER KICK ASS DAY!

I'M SO GLAD I DIDN'T FUCKING DO THIS TODAY.....

DICKHEAD OF THE DAY

HOW MANY PEOPLE PISSED ME OFF TODAY?

(CIRCLE A CUPCAKE FOR EACH PERSON)

 ## NOTES & SHIT

I'M SO FUCKING PROUD OF MYSELF FOR THIS.....

IF TODAY SUCKED...LET THAT SHIT GO!

ONE GOOD
FUCKING THING
THAT HAPPENED
TODAY IS ....

DATE: _____

I AM SO
FUCKING
GRATEFUL FOR

_____

_____

_____

_____

_____

SHIT I HAVE
TO DO TODAY

- [ ] _____
- [ ] _____
- [ ] _____
- [ ] _____
- [ ] _____
- [ ] _____

ANOTHER KICK ASS DAY!

I'M SO GLAD I DIDN'T FUCKING DO THIS TODAY .....

BITCH OF THE DAY

_____
_____
_____
_____

HOW MANY PEOPLE PISSED ME OFF TODAY?

(CIRCLE A CUPCAKE FOR EACH PERSON)

♥ NOTES & SHIT

_____
_____
_____
_____
_____
_____
_____
_____
_____
_____
_____

I'M SO FUCKING PROUD OF MYSELF FOR THIS.....

DON'T WORRY. BE FUCKING HAPPY AND SHIT!

ONE GOOD
FUCKING THING
THAT HAPPENED
TODAY IS ....

DATE: _____

I AM SO
FUCKING
GRATEFUL FOR

_____
_____
_____
_____
_____

SHIT I HAVE
TO DO TODAY

- [ ] _____
- [ ] _____
- [ ] _____
- [ ] _____
- [ ] _____
- [ ] _____

ANOTHER KICK ASS DAY!

I'M SO GLAD I DIDN'T FUCKING DO THIS TODAY.....

ASSHOLE OF THE DAY

_____
_____
_____
_____

HOW MANY PEOPLE PISSED ME OFF TODAY?

(CIRCLE A CUPCAKE FOR EACH PERSON)

 NOTES & SHIT

_____
_____
_____
_____
_____
_____
_____
_____
_____
_____
_____

I'M SO FUCKING PROUD OF MYSELF FOR THIS.....

GET OUT THERE TOMORROW AND MAKE LIFE YOUR BITCH!

ONE GOOD
FUCKING THING
THAT HAPPENED
TODAY IS ....

DATE: _____

I AM SO FUCKING GRATEFUL FOR

SHIT I HAVE TO DO TODAY

- [ ]
- [ ]
- [ ]
- [ ]
- [ ]
- [ ]

ANOTHER KICK ASS DAY!

I'M SO GLAD I DIDN'T FUCKING DO THIS TODAY.....

JERK OF THE DAY

HOW MANY PEOPLE PISSED ME OFF TODAY?

(CIRCLE A CUPCAKE FOR EACH PERSON)

♥ NOTES & SHIT

I'M SO FUCKING PROUD OF MYSELF FOR THIS.....

YOU'RE AMAZING. KEEP THAT SHIT UP!

DATE: _____

I AM SO FUCKING GRATEFUL FOR

_____

_____

_____

_____

SHIT I HAVE TO DO TODAY

- ☐ _____
- ☐ _____
- ☐ _____
- ☐ _____
- ☐ _____
- ☐ _____

ANOTHER KICK ASS DAY!

I'M SO GLAD I DIDN'T FUCKING DO THIS TODAY .....

JACKASS OF THE DAY

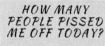

HOW MANY PEOPLE PISSED ME OFF TODAY?

(CIRCLE A CUPCAKE FOR EACH PERSON)

 # NOTES & SHIT

I'M SO FUCKING PROUD OF MYSELF FOR THIS.....

FUCK THIS SHIT SHOW!

DATE: _____

I AM SO FUCKING GRATEFUL FOR

_____

_____

_____

_____

SHIT I HAVE TO DO TODAY

- [ ] _____
- [ ] _____
- [ ] _____
- [ ] _____
- [ ] _____
- [ ] _____

ANOTHER KICK ASS DAY!

I'M SO GLAD I DIDN'T FUCKING DO THIS TODAY .....

BITCH OF THE DAY

HOW MANY PEOPLE PISSED ME OFF TODAY?

(CIRCLE A CUPCAKE FOR EACH PERSON)

♥ ## NOTES & SHIT

I'M SO FUCKING PROUD OF MYSELF FOR THIS.....

DON'T WORRY. BE FUCKING HAPPY AND SHIT!

DATE: _____

I AM SO FUCKING GRATEFUL FOR

_____
_____
_____
_____
_____

SHIT I HAVE TO DO TODAY

- [ ] _____
- [ ] _____
- [ ] _____
- [ ] _____
- [ ] _____
- [ ] _____

ANOTHER KICK ASS DAY!

I'M SO GLAD I DIDN'T FUCKING DO THIS TODAY .....

DICKHEAD OF THE DAY

HOW MANY PEOPLE PISSED ME OFF TODAY?

(CIRCLE A CUPCAKE FOR EACH PERSON)

♥ *NOTES & SHIT*

I'M SO FUCKING PROUD OF MYSELF FOR THIS.....

IF TODAY SUCKED...LET THAT SHIT GO!

ONE GOOD
FUCKING THING
THAT HAPPENED
TODAY IS ....

DATE: _____

I AM SO
FUCKING
GRATEFUL FOR

_____
_____
_____
_____

SHIT I HAVE
TO DO TODAY

- [ ] _____
- [ ] _____
- [ ] _____
- [ ] _____
- [ ] _____
- [ ] _____

ANOTHER KICK ASS DAY!

I'M SO GLAD I DIDN'T FUCKING DO THIS TODAY .....

BITCH OF THE DAY

HOW MANY PEOPLE PISSED ME OFF TODAY?

(CIRCLE A CUPCAKE FOR EACH PERSON)

 # NOTES & SHIT

I'M SO FUCKING PROUD OF MYSELF FOR THIS.....

DON'T WORRY. BE FUCKING HAPPY AND SHIT!

ONE GOOD FUCKING THING THAT HAPPENED TODAY IS ....

DATE: _____

I AM SO FUCKING GRATEFUL FOR

_____

_____

_____

_____

_____

SHIT I HAVE TO DO TODAY

- [ ] _____
- [ ] _____
- [ ] _____
- [ ] _____
- [ ] _____
- [ ] _____

ANOTHER KICK ASS DAY!

I'M SO GLAD I DIDN'T FUCKING DO THIS TODAY .....

ASSHOLE OF THE DAY

HOW MANY PEOPLE PISSED ME OFF TODAY?

(CIRCLE A CUPCAKE FOR EACH PERSON)

 NOTES & SHIT

I'M SO FUCKING PROUD OF MYSELF FOR THIS.....

GET OUT THERE TOMORROW AND MAKE LIFE YOUR BITCH!

ONE GOOD
FUCKING THING
THAT HAPPENED
TODAY IS ....

DATE: _____

I AM SO
FUCKING
GRATEFUL FOR

_____
_____
_____
_____
_____

SHIT I HAVE
TO DO TODAY

- [ ] _____
- [ ] _____
- [ ] _____
- [ ] _____
- [ ] _____
- [ ] _____

ANOTHER KICK ASS DAY!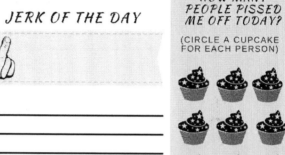

I'M SO GLAD I DIDN'T FUCKING DO THIS TODAY.....

JERK OF THE DAY

HOW MANY PEOPLE PISSED ME OFF TODAY?

(CIRCLE A CUPCAKE FOR EACH PERSON)

 # NOTES & SHIT

I'M SO FUCKING PROUD OF MYSELF FOR THIS.....

YOU'RE AMAZING. KEEP THAT SHIT UP!

ONE GOOD
FUCKING THING
THAT HAPPENED
TODAY IS ....

DATE: _____

I AM SO FUCKING GRATEFUL FOR

_____
_____
_____
_____

SHIT I HAVE TO DO TODAY

☐ _____
☐ _____
☐ _____
☐ _____
☐ _____
☐ _____

ANOTHER KICK ASS DAY!

I'M SO GLAD I DIDN'T FUCKING DO THIS TODAY .....

JACKASS OF THE DAY

_____
_____
_____

HOW MANY PEOPLE PISSED ME OFF TODAY?

(CIRCLE A CUPCAKE FOR EACH PERSON)

♥ NOTES & SHIT

_____
_____
_____
_____
_____
_____
_____
_____
_____
_____

FUCK THIS SHIT SHOW!

I'M SO FUCKING PROUD OF MYSELF FOR THIS.....

ONE GOOD
FUCKING THING
THAT HAPPENED
TODAY IS ....

DATE: _____

I AM SO
FUCKING
GRATEFUL FOR

_____

_____

_____

_____

SHIT I HAVE
TO DO TODAY

☐ _____

☐ _____

☐ _____

☐ _____

☐ _____

☐ _____

ANOTHER KICK ASS DAY!

I'M SO GLAD I DIDN'T FUCKING DO THIS TODAY .....

ASSHOLE OF THE DAY

HOW MANY PEOPLE PISSED ME OFF TODAY?

(CIRCLE A CUPCAKE FOR EACH PERSON)

 NOTES & SHIT

I'M SO FUCKING PROUD OF MYSELF FOR THIS.....

GET OUT THERE TOMORROW AND MAKE LIFE YOUR BITCH!

ONE GOOD
FUCKING THING
THAT HAPPENED
TODAY IS ....

DATE: _____

I AM SO FUCKING GRATEFUL FOR

_____
_____
_____
_____
_____

SHIT I HAVE TO DO TODAY

☐ _____
☐ _____
☐ _____
☐ _____
☐ _____
☐ _____

ANOTHER KICK ASS DAY!

I'M SO GLAD I DIDN'T FUCKING DO THIS TODAY .....

DICKHEAD OF THE DAY

_____
_____
_____
_____

HOW MANY PEOPLE PISSED ME OFF TODAY?

(CIRCLE A CUPCAKE FOR EACH PERSON)

 # NOTES & SHIT

_____
_____
_____
_____
_____
_____
_____
_____
_____
_____
_____

I'M SO FUCKING PROUD OF MYSELF FOR THIS.....

IF TODAY SUCKED...LET THAT SHIT GO!

ONE GOOD
FUCKING THING
THAT HAPPENED
TODAY IS ....

DATE: _____

I AM SO
FUCKING
GRATEFUL FOR

_____
_____
_____
_____

SHIT I HAVE
TO DO TODAY

☐ _____
☐ _____
☐ _____
☐ _____
☐ _____
☐ _____

ANOTHER KICK ASS DAY!

I'M SO GLAD I DIDN'T FUCKING DO THIS TODAY .....

BITCH OF THE DAY

HOW MANY PEOPLE PISSED ME OFF TODAY?

(CIRCLE A CUPCAKE FOR EACH PERSON)

♥ NOTES & SHIT

I'M SO FUCKING PROUD OF MYSELF FOR THIS.....

DON'T WORRY. BE FUCKING HAPPY AND SHIT!

ONE GOOD FUCKING THING THAT HAPPENED TODAY IS ......

DATE: _____

I AM SO FUCKING GRATEFUL FOR

_____
_____
_____
_____

SHIT I HAVE TO DO TODAY

- [ ] _____
- [ ] _____
- [ ] _____
- [ ] _____
- [ ] _____
- [ ] _____

ANOTHER KICK ASS DAY!

I'M SO GLAD I DIDN'T FUCKING DO THIS TODAY .....

ASSHOLE OF THE DAY

HOW MANY PEOPLE PISSED ME OFF TODAY?

(CIRCLE A CUPCAKE FOR EACH PERSON)

 # NOTES & SHIT

I'M SO FUCKING PROUD OF MYSELF FOR THIS.....

GET OUT THERE TOMORROW AND MAKE LIFE YOUR BITCH!

DATE: _____

I AM SO FUCKING GRATEFUL FOR

_____

_____

_____

_____

_____

SHIT I HAVE TO DO TODAY

☐ _____

☐ _____

☐ _____

☐ _____

☐ _____

☐ _____

ANOTHER KICK ASS DAY!

I'M SO GLAD I DIDN'T FUCKING DO THIS TODAY .....

JERK OF THE DAY

HOW MANY PEOPLE PISSED ME OFF TODAY?

(CIRCLE A CUPCAKE FOR EACH PERSON)

♥ NOTES & SHIT

I'M SO FUCKING PROUD OF MYSELF FOR THIS.....

YOU'RE AMAZING. KEEP THAT SHIT UP!

Made in the USA
Middletown, DE
06 December 2022